# THE POETICAL CAT

# THE POETICAL CAT

*An Anthology*

## EDITED BY FELICITY BAST

*Illustrations*
*by*
ROBERT CLYDE ANDERSON

FARRAR STRAUS GIROUX

*New York*

*Copyright information and acknowledgments are continued on page 142.*

# CONTENTS

# CAT ON A STELA

*(from the Stela of Nebra, 1580 B.C.E.,*
*New Kingdom, Egypt)*

The beautiful cat which endures, endures.

# PREFACE

*Kattos, aigulous, neko, Katze, gatto, kuching, felis, cait, chat, cat.* Cats as domestic animals stalk the globe, East to West, collecting not only their owners but also the poets whom they've served as muses virtually from the day they consented to leave desert, thicket, and barn for temple, cottage, and palace, to live with human beings.

Our affection for cats is a complicated one, since we feel compelled to love an animal whose very character is a constellation of paradoxes. The adorable kitten becomes a feral hunter; the companionable friend is known to go its own solitary and skittish way, spurning accountability to anyone; the soft and purring habitué of laps, pillows, and hearthrugs becomes, in a leap, the merciless assassin of innocent chipmunks, voles, wrens, newts, bats: for the country cat, lawn, field, and wood are jungles stocked with tiny prey, while the city cat proclaims its urbanity with a menu only slightly more constrained, emphasizing birds and mice, disdaining cockroaches in favor of the blameless grasshopper.

Celebrated for their decorum, delicacy, and grace, cats fling these exquisite qualities to the wind when mating: they yowl, fight, roll around, and arch their backs with such an obscene voluptuousness as to make voyeurs of us all, and we wonder at the extravagance of their erotic lives while considering with dismay the hopeless demographics of their offspring.

So they court, they nurture, they sleuth, and they sleep; they disappear and return, explore ceaselessly, yet hug the familiar, and hold up so remorseless a reflection of ourselves in their agate eyes that it is never clear, even to the most devoted and knowledgeable of cat owners, whether we anthropomorphize their alien felineness or, indeed, they mirror our own traits, from the darkest to the most endearing. Their affections seem almost arbitrary; their loyalties, whether in their sensual lives or in the sphere of their human attachments, capricious. Their lives, as anyone who has ever kept and lost a cat can testify, seem much too brief to encompass the range of behaviors and experience with which they decorate our own. The grief we feel at losing them—to traffic, to a dog, to a particularly vicious cat fight, or to the advances of illness and age that leave them smaller, thinner, and finally curled into a comma of fur in a corner of the room—may seem excessive to those who have never been companions to a cat, but it is real and wrenching.

The attractiveness of cats to poets has been enduring, from the Egyptian New Kingdom (though there is a singular absence of tributes to cats in the Bible) through the medieval monasteries of Celtic Ireland and the salons of the French *ancien régime*. Why has this small creature, a lion in miniature, a lesser deity in a number of cultures, exerted such a strong tug of fascination and allure that poets pick up their pens in homage to them? Perhaps it's because they embody paradox so deliciously (paradox is to poet as mouse to cat); perhaps the stereotyped limitation of their repertoire of behaviors attracts the formalist who loves the romp of freedom within the necessity of the set piece, the play of wild imagination within the constraints of tameness and order. Or, finally, perhaps it is their secrecy, the sense of the enigmatic and the unknowable, that fires these poems: Robert Graves has remarked on their sacredness to the moon goddess, noting their similarities. Cats' eyes shine in the dark; they feed on mice, which are symbols of pestilence; they mate openly but walk silently; they are maternal and prolific, but do, alas, sometimes eat their young; and finally, he remarks that their colors vary, like the moon in different seasons, ranging from white to ginger red to all the shades of black.

From the outset I did not intend this to become a "Complete Book of Cat Poems" but have attempted instead, with feline fastidiousness, to make this a *highly selective* book of poems about cats. A number of famous chestnuts have been brusquely excluded, displaced by poems with which, exotic though some of them may seem, I felt instantly at home. There are poems here in which feline traits are highly allegorized (the medieval Persian "Gorby and the Rats," for example, as well as La Fontaine). Some, from sources as disparate as medieval China and early-twentieth-century Britain, focus on the Bad Cat (the mutual seductions of our two species are complicated indeed); a few craftily invoke the cat as a metaphor for the human condition. But despite the ubiquity of subject—"the beautiful cat which endures"—the poems are remarkably individual. Just so, as all cat owners understand, every cat is unique, a personality in its own exquisite right, as beautiful, knowable, and yet ultimately mysterious as a good poem.

**Note:** *Poems designated as being "after" a source are free translations, sometimes translations in verse of prose originals, by the editor.*

# THE POETICAL CAT

# THE SINGING CAT

*Stevie Smith (1902–71)*

It was a little captive cat
    Upon a crowded train
His mistress takes him from his box
    To ease his fretful pain.

She holds him tight upon her knee
    The graceful animal
And all the people look at him
    He is so beautiful.

But oh he pricks and oh he prods
    And turns upon her knee
Then lifteth up his innocent voice
    In plaintive melody.

He lifteth up his innocent voice
    He lifteth up, he singeth
And to each human countenance
    A smile of grace he bringeth.

He lifteth up his innocent paw
    Upon her breast he clingeth
And everybody cries, Behold
    The cat, the cat that singeth.

He lifteth up his innocent voice
    He lifteth up, he singeth
And all the people warm themselves
    In the love his beauty bringeth.

# THE CAT AND THE LUTE

*Thomas Master (1603–43)*

Are these the strings that poets say
Have cleared the air, and calmed the sea?
Charmed wolves, and from the mountain crests
Made forests dance with all their beasts?
Could these neglected shreds you see
Inspire a lute of ivory
And make it speak? Oh! think then what
Hath been committed by my cat,
Who, in the silence of this night
Hath gnawed these cords, and ruined them quite,
Leaving such remnants as may be
"Frets"—not for my lute, but me.

Puss, I will curse thee; mayest thou dwell
With some dry hermit in a cell
Where rat ne'er peeped, where mouse ne'er fed,
And flies go supperless to bed.
Or may'st thou tumble from some tower,
And fail to land upon all fours,
Taking a fall that may untie
Eight of nine lives, and let them fly.

What, was there ne'er a rat nor mouse,
Nor larder open? nought in the house
But harmless lute-strings could suffice
Thy paunch, and draw thy glaring eyes?

Know then, thou wretch, that every string
Is a cat-gut, which men do spin
Into a singing thread: think on that,
Thou cannibal, thou monstrous cat!

Thou seest, puss, what evil might betide thee:
But I forbear to hurt or chide thee:

For maybe puss was melancholy
And so to make her blithe and jolly,
Finding these strings, she took a snatch
Of merry music: nay then, wretch,
Thus I revenge me, that as thou
Hast played on them, I've played on you.

# THE CAT

*Nguyen Trai (1380–1442)*

Well, cat, did you find enlightenment in the Western Paradise?
You serve the Buddha well, unseen by the temple monks.
In the kitchen you hang about, while the dog gets kicked out.
You could even teach tricks to a tiger, though he still can't
     climb trees.
Does anyone know how to keep you out of a room,
Or to stop you from making a meal whenever you feel like it?
Truly you are a dreadful bother, but we give you a home:
Because we loathe mice, we put up with the likes of you.

*—translated from the Vietnamese
by Jess Williamson*

# CONCORD CATS

*Richard Eberhart (1904–    )*


The soft cat and the scratchy cat
Have milk in cold blue plates.
Then, in evenings, star-cool evenings
Equal to their reticence,
Emblems of independence,

These China cats, of black and white,
Will go on planetary pads
Uphill, where crouch
On eighteenth-, seventeenth-century
Houses the graves of Concord.

By pious inscriptions
That antedate the Revolution
They see, through eyes cold and chaste,
The scratchy cat, the soft cat,
With humor old and Oriental,

That nature is meant for poise.
Battles, bloodshed, death,
And men mirroring time,—
The stars blue, the night paling—
Are data.   Imperviousness.   Integrity.

# THE EGYPTIAN CAT

*D. J. Enright (1920–    )*

How harsh the change, since those plump halcyon days
                beneath the chair of Nakht—
Posed in conscious humour above the prostrate fish,
No backstairs bones, no scraped and sorry skeleton,
                no death's-head
From a toppled dustbin, but sacred unity of fish
                and flesh and spirit—
With its stately fantail, its fiery markings like your own,
As tiger-god found good its tiger-offering . . .
For your seat is now among beggars, and neither man
                nor cat is longer honoured,
As you with your lank ribs slink, and he
                sprawls among his stumps.
Young boys, they say, lay their limbs on tram-lines
                to enter this hard métier—
But you, maddened among the gross cars, mocked by klaxons,
Lie at last in the gutter merely and clearly dead . . .

And so I think of the old days—you strong and a little malignant,
Bent like a bow, like a rainbow proud in colour,
Tense on your tail's taut spring, at Thebes—
Where Death reigned over pharaohs, and by dark arts
Cast a light and lasting beauty over life itself—you
Templed beneath the chair, tearing a fresh and virgin fish.

# TO A CAT

*Algernon Charles Swinburne (1837–1909)*

Stately, kindly, lordly friend,
   Condescend
Here to sit by me, and turn
Glorious eyes that smile and burn,
Golden eyes, love's lustrous meed,
On the golden page I read.

All your wondrous wealth of hair,
   Dark and fair,
Silken-shaggy, soft and bright
As the clouds and beams of night,
Pays my reverent hand's caress
Back with friendlier gentleness.

Dogs may fawn on all and some
   As they come;
You, a friend of loftier mind,
Answer friends alone in kind.
Just your foot upon my hand
Softly bids it understand.

# PROPRIETY

*Kawai Chigetsu-ni (1632–1736)*

Cats making love in the temple
But people would blame
A man and wife for mating in such a place.

—*translated from the Japanese
by Kenneth Rexroth and Ikuko Atsumi*

# THE CAT AND THE MOON

*William Butler Yeats (1865–1939)*

The cat went here and there
And the moon spun round like a top,
And the nearest kin of the moon,
The creeping cat, looked up.
Black Minnaloushe stared at the moon,
For, wander and wail as he would,
The pure cold light in the sky
Troubled his animal blood.
Minnaloushe runs in the grass
Lifting his delicate feet.
Do you dance, Minnaloushe, do you dance?
When two close kindred meet,
What better than call a dance?
Maybe the moon may learn,
Tired of that courtly fashion,
A new dance turn.
Minnaloushe creeps through the grass
From moonlit place to place,
The sacred moon overhead
Has taken a new phase.
Does Minnaloushe know that his pupils
Will pass from change to change,
And that from round to crescent,
From crescent to round they range?
Minnaloushe creeps through the grass
Alone, important and wise,
And lifts to the changing moon
His changing eye.

# CHRYSOBERYL: THE EYE OF THE CAT

*after Plutarch (46–120 C.E.)*

The Egyptians, in the worship of Isis, played the *sistrum*, or timbrel, during their ceremonies—a musical and mystical instrument whose arched top displayed the image of a female cat, *couchant* (from Plutarch's *Moralia* 1312: The Eye of the Cat).

At the crest of the arch of the timbrel
they engrave a cat.
Her face (shadow of the Sphinx!)
is human.
She recalls
in her pied color
her nocturnal ways
and in her fecundity
(for they say she brings forth one,
then two,
then three,
then four,
up to five at one birth,
and can add by one
up to seven
to her litter,
producing all in all eight-and-twenty young,
equal in number to)
the phases of the moon.

A fable, you say.
But surely
the pupils of her eyes
wax, dilate
when the moon is full
and narrow and dull
when it wanes.
No one at all has any doubt of this:
for the cat with her Human Countenance
expresses best the Intelligence
and the Rationality (Sovereign Reason, the Great Queen!)
of the Changes of the Moon.

*—F.B.*

# PUSSYCAT SITS ON A CHAIR

*Edward Newman Horn (1903–76)*


Pussycat sits on a chair
Implacably with acid stare.

Those who early loved in vain
Use the cat to try again,

And test their bruised omnipotence
Against the cat's austere defense.

# THE KITTEN

*Ogden Nash (1902–71)*

The trouble with a kitten is
THAT
Eventually it becomes a
CAT.

# HYWEL THE GOOD
# WEIGHS THE WORTH OF A CAT

*after the* Code of North Wales *(936)*

The worth of a cat and her c-
    attributes is as follows:

Primus:      The worth of a kitten from the night
          it is kittened until it shall open its eyes is a legal
          penny.

Secundus:  And from that time, until it shall slay mice,
          two legal pence:

Tertius:    And after it shall kill mice, four legal pence, and so it shall remain,
          *prix fixe.*

Her *attributes* are the powers:
      (Item) to see,
      (Item) to hear,
      (Item) to kill mice,
      (Item) to have her claws entire

and NOT devour her kittens,

And if she be bought, and lack any one of these *attributes*,

There's a refund: a third of your money back.

—F.B.

# THE GREATER CATS

*Vita Sackville-West (1892–1962)*

The greater cats with golden eyes
Stare out between the bars.
Deserts are there and different skies,
And night with different stars.
They prowl the aromatic hill,
And mate as fiercely as they kill,
And hold the freedom of their will
To roam, to live, to drink their fill;
But this beyond their wit know I:
Man loves a little, and for long shall die.

Their kind across the desert range
Where tulips spring from stones,
Not knowing they will suffer change
Or vultures pick their bones.
Their strength's eternal in their sight,
They rule the terror of the night,
They overtake the deer in flight,
And in their arrogance they smite;
But I am sage, if they are strong:
Man's love is transient as his death is long.

Yet oh what powers to deceive!
My wit is turned to faith,
And at this moment I believe
In love, and scout at death.
I came from nowhere, and shall be
Strong, steadfast, swift, eternally:
I am a lion, a stone, a tree,
And as the Polar star in me
Is fixed my constant heart on thee.
Ah, may I stay forever blind
With lions, tigers, leopards, and their kind.

# MUJER

*William Carlos Williams (1883–1963)*


Oh, black Persian cat!
Was not your life
already cursed with offspring?
We took you for rest to that old
Yankee farm,—so lonely
and with so many field mice
in the long grass—
and you return to us
in this condition—!

Oh, black Persian cat.

# CHANG TUAN'S CATS

*after Wang Chih (c. 1100 C.E.)*

Scholar Chang Tuan was fond of cats,
And had seven of them,
Wonderful beasts with wonderful names.
They were:
>Guardian of the East
>White Phoenix
>Purple Blossom
>Drive-Away-Vexation
>Brocade Sash
>Cloud Pattern
>Ten Thousand Strings of Cash

Each was worth several pieces of gold,
And nothing could persuade Chang
To part with them.

>*—F.B.*

# NEBAMUN'S CAT

*after a fresco from the Middle Kingdom, Egypt (c. 2600–2500 B.C.E.)*

"A favorite cat sometimes attended them on these occasions [fowling excursions]; and from the readiness with which it is represented to have seized the game, the artist has intended to show those animals acted as retrievers, or were trained to catch the birds; being let out of the boat into the thickets which grew at the water's edge."

—*J. Gardner Wilkinson*
Customs and Manners of the Ancient Egyptians,
*1878*

Taking recreation, seeing pleasant things,
    and
        occupying
            himself
                with
                    the
                        craft
                          of
            THE MARSH GODDESS
the lady of sport adores him
and even this scribe
who keeps track of the grain in the silos
sings his praises,
I, Nebamun.

—*F.B.*

# THE SONG OF THE CAT

*Tristan Klingsor (1874–1966)*

Cat, cat, cat,
Cat black, or white, or grey,
You look pretty curled up like that—
But cat—cat, cat,
Can't you hear the mice at play
Dancing a cheeky roundelay
Under the floor of your very own flat?

The landlord snores upon his pillow
(A cotton nightcap warms his pate),
While a glassy moon unseen, outside
Shines softly through the window grate.

Mice, step lively, now's your chance,
Dance a jolly, free-form dance;
Patter paws to tuneless ditties,
Flick your tails about and dance
A moon-lit fairy-ring

But fast! The city
Wardens in the street
Are pounding pavements on their beat,
While every Paris cat's asleep:
Each cat upon its proper mat,
A white, or black, or grey house-cat.

*—translated from the French*
*by F.B.*

# MOONLIGHT

*attributed to Rajasekhara (c. seventh century C.E.)*

The cat at his dish licks rays of moonlight
    because he thinks them milk
and where they weave among the branches of trees,
    the elephant sees his food of white lotus stems.
The woman who has just made love reaches out
    for the moonlight on her bed as if for her sheer dress.
How the moon in his pride, drunk with his own light,
    confuses the currents of this world!

                  *—translated from the Sanskrit*
                    *by Henry Heifetz*

# JUSTICE

*Agathias (536–82)*


You expect, Puss-in-Boots
    to go on treating my house
as your house
    after treating my pet partridge
as a comestible?

No, pet partridge!
Over the bones of his treat
    the cat shall be slain,
and you honored in blood rite:
as Pyrrhus, recall,
(rightfully) slew
    Polyxena
over the corpse of Achilles.

              *—translated from the Greek*
              *by Peter Whigham*

# THE CAT TO HIS DINNER

*Nancy Willard (1936–    )*

Fern and flower, safely keep
this tender mouse I put to sleep.

Let snow and silence mark the site
of my unseemly appetite.

Her bravery, her tiny fall
shall be a model for us all.

May God, Who knows our best and worst,
send me another as good as the first.

# THE CAT'S EYE

*Yorie (1884–1941)*

In the eyes of the cat
Is the color of the sea,
On a sunny day, in winter.

# THE CAT

*Kusatao (1901–83)*

Flourishing his head around
He licks himself smooth and sleek—
The moonlight cat!

> —*translated from the Japanese
> by Tze-si Huang*

# THE SCHOLAR AND THE CAT

*Anonymous (ninth century, C.E.)*

Each of us pursues his trade,
I and Pangur my comrade,
His whole fancy on the hunt,
And mine for learning ardent.

More than fame I love to be
Among my books and study,
Pangur does not grudge me it,
Content with his own merit.

When—a heavenly time!—we are
In our small room together
Each of us has his own sport
And asks no greater comfort.

While he sets his round sharp eye
On the walls of my study
I turn mine, though lost its edge
On the great wall of knowledge.

Now a mouse drops in his net
After some mighty onset
While into my bag I cram
Some difficult darksome problem.

When a mouse comes to the kill
Pangur exults, a marvel!
I have when some secret's won
My hour of exaltation.

Though we work for days and years
Neither the other hinders;
Each is competent and hence
Enjoys his skill in silence.

Master of the death of mice,
He keeps in daily practice,
I too, making dark things clear,
Am of my trade a master.

*—translated from the Irish*
*by Frank O'Connor*

# TO MRS. PROFESSOR
# IN DEFENSE OF MY CAT'S HONOR
# AND NOT ONLY

*Czeslaw Milosz (1911– )*

My valiant helper, a small-sized tiger
Sleeps sweetly on my desk, by the computer,
Unaware that you insult his tribe.

Cats play with a mouse or with a half-dead mole.
You are wrong, though: it's not out of cruelty.
They simply like a thing that moves.

For, after all, we know that only consciousness
Can for a moment move into the Other,
Empathize with the pain and panic of a mouse.

And such as cats are, all of Nature is.
Indifferent, alas, to the good and the evil.
Quite a problem for us, I am afraid.

Natural history has its museums,
But why should our children learn about monsters,
An earth of snakes and reptiles for millions of years?

Nature devouring, Nature devoured,
Butchery day and night smoking with blood.
And who created it? Was it the good Lord?

Yes, undoubtedly, they are innocent,
Spiders, mantises, sharks, pythons.
We are the only ones who say: cruelty.

Our consciousness and our conscience
Alone in the pale anthill of galaxies
Put their hope in a humane God.

Who cannot but feel and think,
Who is kindred to us by His warmth and movement,
For we are, as He told us, similar to Him.

Yet if it is so, then He takes pity
On every mauled mouse, every wounded bird.
Then the universe for Him is like a Crucifixion.

Such is the outcome of your attack on the cat:
A theological, Augustinian grimace,
Which makes difficult our walking on this earth.

*—translated from the Polish*
*by the author and Robert Hass*

# CATS

*Charles Baudelaire (1821–67)*

They are alike, prim scholar and perfervid lover:
When comes the season of decay, they both decide
Upon sweet, husky cats to be the household pride;
Cats choose, like them, to sit, and like them, shudder.

Like partisans of carnal dalliance, and science,
They search for silence and the shadowings of dread;
Hell well might harness them as horses for the dead,
If it could bend their native proudness in compliance.

In reverie they emulate the noble mood
Of giant sphinxes stretched in depths of solitude
Who seem to slumber in a never-ending dream;

Within their fertile loins a sparkling magic lies;
Finer than any sand are dusts of gold that gleam,
Vague starpoints, in the mystic iris of their eyes.

*—translated from the French*
*by William H. Crosby*

# CHILDREN'S SONG

*Anonymous*


Cock-a-doodle-doo! I want my leftover rice!
Where is my leftover rice?
The cat ate it all up.
Where is the cat?
She went to chase a rat.
Where is the rat?
It ran into a hole.
Where is the hole?
The cow trampled it shut.
Where is the cow?
The river carried her away.
Where is the river?
It has all dried up.

—*after a translation from the Nepalese*
*by Kumar Prakesh*

# AN OFFERING FOR THE CAT

*Mei Yao-ch'en (1002–60)*

Since I got my cat Five White
the rats never bother my books.
This morning Five White died.
I make offerings of rice and fish,
bury you in mid-river
with incantations—I wouldn't slight you.
Once you caught a rat,
ran round the garden with it squeaking in your mouth;
you hoped to put a scare into the other rats,
to clean up my house.
When we'd come aboard the boat
you shared our cabin,
and though we'd nothing but meager dried rations,
we ate them without fear of rat piss and gnawing—
because you were diligent,
a good deal more so than the pigs and chickens.
People make much of their prancing steeds;
they tell me nothing can compare to a horse or donkey—
Enough!—I'll argue the point no longer,
only cry for you a little.

> —*translated from the Chinese*
> *by Burton Watson*

# F R O M  EPITAPH FOR BELAUD

*Joachim Du Bellay (1522–60)*


. . . There are cats (not he)
Who night and day are on the prowl,
The belly is their only law:
But Belaud was a thrifty pet
Who kept his mealtimes quite discreet,
Frugal, delicate, and neat.
There are cats (not he)
Who parade their prey:
A trail of bodies everywhere
Meets your eye, perfumes the air
But Belaud was a gentle soul
A decent beast who kept his caches
Of tiny corpses beneath the ashes.
A toy, the finest of bijoux
His trade forever to amuse
Perched upon the spinning wheel
Muttering his threnody
In tune with its monotony:
Composing his sweet rondel
At the highest pitch of caterwaul.

Blameless Belaud! His only crime
To patrol my nights too zealously
To watch my bed so jealously
Lest midnight rats disturb my rest
Great Belaud would give them chase:
A leap, a pounce, a snarling snap—
None escaped his watchful trap.
. . .
Please God, in this remembrance
Of the finest cat in France
May I have the wit, the style, the force
To herald this great aristocrat
In verse as fair as my Beau Chat:
Live on, Belaud! For you'll endure
While cats keep the world from rats secure.

*—translated from the French
by F.B.*

# SIX LITTLE MICE

*Mother Goose (seventeenth century)*

Six little mice sat down to spin;
Pussy passed by and she peeped in.
What are you doing, my little men?
Weaving coats for gentlemen.
Shall I come in and cut off your threads?
No, no, Mistress Pussy, you'd bite off our heads.
Oh, no, I'll not; I'll help you to spin.
That may be so, but you can't come in.
Says Puss: You look so wondrous wise,
I like your whiskers and bright black eyes;
Your house is the nicest house I see,
I think there is room for you and for me.
The mice were so pleased that they opened the door,
And Pussy soon had them all dead on the floor.

# THE CAT CHANGED TO A WOMAN

*Jean de La Fontaine (1621–95)*

A man one time became dementedly fond of his cat—
The silkiest, daintiest, most exquisite, he thought.
        Indeed the mere sound of her miaow
        Thrilled him until he had somehow,
    By tears and prayers of a touched brain,
        Forged potent forces of a chain,
        As only sorcery could have done,
        And transformed his cat, when the links were one,
        To an actual woman, at dawn, in the room!
        Our Merlin wed her that very day
        And ecstatic folly reversed the gloom
        Of ill-starred love—sickness, I'd say.
        No temptress really beautiful
        Charmed man so easily
        As this strange wife her marital fool
        Who had been brooding constantly.
        He saw no trace of cat to regret,
But while gnawing a mat that night, mice were a threat
To the peaceful sleep of the newly wed.
        The enchanted cat by a dart from bed
        Missed the mice she inferred were near,
Crouched forward since certain that they would reappear,
    And next time took them by surprise;
        For having discerned no form to fear,
        They had not avoided her disguise.
        Her weakness remained a curse of course;
        Such is Nature's interior force.

Instinct scorns rebukes when one has reached maturity.
The fold is in the goods; a scent haunts the vase perpetually.

Deflecting nature is absurd
From whatever course it has pursued.
Bring pressure to bear but rest assured
Matters will stand just where they stood.
Prod habit with pitchforks however hard,
It behaves as if nothing had occurred.
Or beat with leather till it's a shred.
You've tried to reform what will not learn.
Shut doors on traits that you wish were dead;
They will open a window and return.

—*translated from the French
by Marianne Moore*

# CAT

*Lytton Strachey (1880–1932)*

Dear creature by the fire a-purr,
  Strange idol, eminently bland,
Miraculous puss! As o'er your fur
  I trail a negligible hand,

And gaze into your gazing eyes,
  And wonder in a demi-dream,
What mystery it is that lies,
  Behind those slits that glare and gleam,

An exquisite enchantment falls
  About the portals of my sense;
Meandering through enormous halls,
  I breathe luxurious frankincense,

An ampler air, a warmer June
  Enfold me, and my wondering eye
Salutes a more imperial moon
  Throned in a more resplendent sky

Than ever knew this northern shore.
  Oh, strange! For you are with me too,
And I who am a cat once more
  Follow the woman that was you

With tail erect and pompous march,
  The proudest puss that ever trod,
Through many a grove, 'neath many an arch,
  Impenetrable as a god.

Down many an alabaster flight
  Of broad and cedar-shaded stairs,
While over us the elaborate night
  Mysteriously gleams and glares.

# THE CAT AS CAT

*Denise Levertov (1923–   )*

The cat on my bosom
sleeping and purring
—fur-petalled chrysanthemum,
squirrel-killer—

is a metaphor only if I
force him to be one,
looking too long in his pale, fond,
dilating, contracting eyes

that reject mirrors, refuse
to observe what bides
stockstill.
      Likewise

flex and reflex of claws
gently pricking through sweater to skin
gently sustains their own tune
not mine. I-Thou, cat, I-Thou.

# CAT

*Sutardji Calzoum Bachri (1942–    )*

Meow!    There's a cat in my blood    he roars he runs
he hurts    he flows through my aorta in the forest of my
blood    he is enormous but he is not a lion and not a
tiger and not a jaguar and not a leopard but a tabby cat
and not a cat but a CAT    Meow!    he is hungry he
levels the forests of Africa with his claws and madness he
roars he howls don't feed him he doesn't like meat    Jesus
don't give him bread he doesn't like bread    Meow!

a cat fighting in my blood roaring pushing his way through
the coals in my heart he is hungry very hungry    Meow!
he has not eaten for a million days a thousand eons he is
never satisfied very hungry my curious cat perpetually clawing
wait God created the cat I didn't ask Him to he roars in
search of Him    he is hungry    don't feed him flesh feed
him rice God created him I didn't want Him to he wants God to
one day make him tame so he can live in peace with the world

Meow! he roars    how many Gods are there    give me one to
keep my cat quiet    Meow    shush pussy shush    I fix
traps in Africa in the Amazon in Riau in cities    who knows
perhaps I'll catch me a God    not bad    a slice for you
and a slice for me    shush pussy shush    Meow!

—*translated from the Malay*
*by Harry Aveling*

# MY CATS

*Stevie Smith (1902–71)*

I like to toss him up and down
A heavy cat weighs half a Crown
With a hey do diddle my cat Brown.

I like to pinch him on the sly
When nobody is passing by
With a hey do diddle my cat Fry.

I like to ruffle up his pride
And watch him skip and turn aside
With a hey do diddle my cat Hyde.

Hey Brown and Fry and Hyde my cats
That sit on tombstones for your mats.

# THE BODY OF THE GREAT CAT

*after the "Seventy-Five Praises of Ra"*
*inscribed on the Royal Tombs at Thebes (c. 1200–1100 B.C.E.)*

All praise to thee, O Ra!
Lord Ra, exalted Sekhem!
Thou art the Great Cat:
    And thus,
      Avenger of the gods;
      And judge of the rightness of words;
      And overlord of magistrates.
You preside over the Holy Circle:
Truly the embodiment of the Great Cat!

          —*F.B.*

# COLD MOUNTAIN POEM NO. 158

*Han Shan (c. 700–80)*

In other days, I was poor enough to suit,
But now I freeze in utter poverty:
I make a deal—it doesn't quite work out,
I take the road—it ends in misery;
I walk in the mud—my feet slip out from under,
I sit in the shrine—my belly gripes at me—
Since I lost the parti-colored cat,
Around the rice-jar, rats wait hungrily.

*—translated from the Chinese*
*by E. Bruce Brooks*

# THE PRAYER OF THE CAT

*Carmen Bernos de Gasztold (twentieth century)*


Lord,
I am the cat.
It is not, exactly, that I have something to ask of You!
No—
I ask nothing of anyone—
but,
if You have by some chance, in some celestial barn,
a little white mouse,
or a saucer of milk,
I know someone who would relish them.
Wouldn't You like someday
to put a curse on the whole race of dogs?
If so I should say,

Amen

*—translated from the Spanish*
*by Rumer Godden*

# FROM JUBILATE AGNO

(A Poem from Bedlam)

*Christopher Smart (1722–71)*

For I will consider my cat Jeoffry.

For he is the servant of the living God, duly and daily serving him.

For at the first glance of the glory of God in the East he worships in his way.

For this is done by wreathing his body seven times round with elegant quickness.

For when he leaps up to catch the musk, which is the blessing of God upon his prayer.

For he rolls upon prank to work it in.

For having done duty and received blessing he begins to consider himself.

For this he performs in ten degrees.

For first he looks upon his fore-paws to see if they are clean.

For secondly he kicks up behind to clear away there.

For thirdly he works it upon stretch with the fore-paws extended.

For fourthly he sharpens his paws by wood.

For fifthly he washes himself.

For sixthly he rolls upon wash.

For seventhly he fleas himself, that he may not be interrupted upon the beat.

For eighthly he rubs himself against a post.

For ninthly he looks up for his instructions.

For tenthly he goes in quest of food.

For having consider'd God and himself he will consider his neighbour.

For if he meets another cat he will kiss her in kindness.

For when he takes his prey he plays with it to give it [a] chance.

For one mouse in seven escapes by his dallying.

For when his day's work is done his business more properly begins.

For he keeps the Lord's watch in the night against the adversary.

For he counteracts the powers of darkness by his electrical skin and glaring eyes.

For he counteracts the Devil, who is death, by brisking about the life.

For in his morning orisons he loves the sun and the sun loves him.

For he is of the tribe of Tiger.

For the Cherub Cat is a term of the Angel Tiger.

For he has the subtlety and hissing of a serpent, which in goodness he suppresses.

For he will not do destruction, if he is well-fed, neither will he spit without provocation.

For he purrs in thankfulness, when God tells him he's a good Cat.

For he is an instrument for the children to learn benevolence upon.

For every house is incompleat without him & a blessing is lacking in the Spirit.

For the Lord commanded Moses concerning the cats at the departure of the Children of Israel from Egypt.

For every family had one cat at least in the bag.

For the English cats are the best in Europe.

For he is the cleanest in the use of his fore-paws of any quadrupeds.

For the dexterity of his defence is an instance of the love of God to him exceedingly.

For he is the quickest to his mark of any creature.

For he is tenacious of his point.

For he is a mixture of gravity and waggery.

For he knows that God is his Saviour.

For there is nothing sweeter than his peace when at rest.

For there is nothing brisker than his life when in motion.

For he is of the Lord's poor and so indeed is he called by benevolence perpetually—Poor Jeoffry! poor Jeoffry! the rat has bit thy throat.

For I bless the name of the Lord Jesus that Jeoffry is better.

For the divine spirit comes about his body to sustain it in compleat cat.

For his tongue is exceeding pure so that it has in purity what it wants in musick.

For he is docile and can learn certain things.

For he can set up with gravity which is patience upon approbation.

For he can fetch and carry, which is patience in employment.

For he can jump over a stick which is patience upon proof positive.

For he can spraggle upon waggle at the word of command.

For he can jump from an eminence into his master's bosom.

For he can catch the cork and toss it again.

For he is hated by the hypocrite and miser.

For the former is afraid of detection.

For the latter refuses the charge.

For he camels his back to bear the first motion of business.

For he is good to think on, if a man would express himself neatly.

For he made a great figure in Egypt for his signal services.

For he killed the Icneumon-rat very pernicious by land.

For his ears are so acute that they sting again.

For from this proceeds the passing quickness of his attention.

For by stroaking of him I have found out electricity.

For I perceived God's light about him both wax and fire.

For the Electrical fire is the spiritual substance, which God sends from heaven to sustain the bodies both of man and beast.

For God has blessed him in the variety of his movements.

For, tho he cannot fly, he is an excellent clamberer.

For his motions upon the face of the earth are more than any other quadrupeds.

For he can tread to all the measures upon the musick.

For he can swim for life.

For he can creep.

# THE CAT

*Issa (1763–1827)*

The cat
sleeps
wakes up
gives one vast yawn then
exits for the purposes of love.

—*translated from the Japanese*
*by Harry Guest*

# AN APPEAL TO CATS
# IN THE BUSINESS OF LOVE

*Thomas Flatman (1637–88)*

Ye cats that at midnight spit love at each other,
Who best feel the pangs of a passionate lover,
I appeal to your scratches and your tattered fur,
If the business of love be no more than to purr.
Old Lady Grimalkin with her gooseberry eyes,
Knew something when a kitten, for why she is wise;
You find by experience, the love-fit's soon o'er,
*Puss! Puss!* lasts not long, but turns to *Cat-whore!*
      Men ride many miles,
      Cats tread many tiles,
    Both hazard their necks in the fray;
        Only cats, when they fall
        From a house or a wall,
    Keep their feet, mount their tails, and away!

# THE OWL AND THE PUSSY~CAT

*Edward Lear (1812–88)*


The Owl and the Pussy-cat went to sea
  In a beautiful pea-green boat,
They took some honey, and plenty of money,
  Wrapped up in a five-pound note.
The Owl looked up to the stars above,
  And sang to a small guitar,
"O lovely Pussy! O Pussy, my love,
  What a beautiful Pussy you are,
    You are,
    You are!
  What a beautiful Pussy you are!"

Pussy said to the Owl, "You elegant fowl!
  How charmingly sweet you sing!
O let us be married! too long we have tarried:
  But what shall we do for a ring?"
They sailed away, for a year and a day,
  To the land where the Bong-Tree grows,
And there in a wood a Piggy-wig stood,
  With a ring at the end of his nose,
    His nose,
    His nose,
  With a ring at the end of his nose.

"Dear Pig, are you willing to sell for one shilling
    Your ring?" Said the Piggy, "I will."
So they took it away, and were married next day
    By the Turkey who lives on the hill.
They dined on mince, and slices of quince,
    Which they ate with a runcible spoon;
And hand in hand, on the edge of the sand,
    They danced by the light of the moon,
        The moon,
        The moon,
    They danced by the light of the moon.

# LE HIBOU ET LA POUSSIQUETTE

*Edward Lear, translated into French*
*by Francis Steegmuller (1906–94)*


Hibou et Minou allèrent à la mer
Dans une barque peinte en jaune-canari;
Ils prirent du miel roux et beaucoup de sous
Enroulés dans une lettre de crédit.
Le hibou contemplait les astres du ciel,
Et chantait, en grattant de sa guitare,
"O Minou chérie, ô Minou ma belle,
O Poussiquette, comme tu es rare,
   Es rare,
   Es rare!
O Poussiquette, comme tu es rare!"


Au chanteur dit la chatte, "Noble sieur à deux pattes,
Votre voix est d'une telle élégance!
Voulez-vous, cher Hibou, devenir mon époux?
Mais que faire pour trouver une alliance?"
Il voguèrent, fous d'amour, une année et un jour;
Puis, au pays où le bong fleurit beau,
Un cochon de lait surgit d'une forêt,
Une bague accrochée au museau.
   Museau,
   Museau,
Une bague accrochée au museau.

"Cochon, veux-tu bien nous vendre pour un rien
Ta bague?" Le cochon consentit.
Donc ils prirent le machin, et le lendemain matin
Le dindon sur le mont les unit.
Ils firent un repas de maigre et de gras,
Se servant d'une cuillère peu commune;
Et là sur la plage, le nouveau ménage
Dansa au clair de la lune,
            La lune,
            La lune,
Dansa au clair de la lune.

# CAT'S DREAM

*Pablo Neruda (1904–73)*

How neatly a cat sleeps,
sleeps with its paws and its posture,
sleeps with its wicked claws,
and with its unfeeling blood,
sleeps with all the rings—
a series of burnt circles—
which have formed the odd geology
of its sand-colored tail.

I should sleep like a cat,
with all the fur of time,
with a tongue rough as flint,
with the dry sex of fire;
and after speaking to no one,
stretch myself over the world,
over the roofs and landscapes,
with a passionate desire
to hunt the rats in my dreams.

I have seen how the cat asleep
would undulate, how the night
flowed through it like dark water;
and at times, it was going to fall
or possibly plunge into
the bare deserted snowdrifts.
Sometimes it grew so much in sleep
like a tiger's great-grandfather,
and would leap in the darkness over
rooftops, clouds and volcanoes.

Sleep, sleep, cat of the night
with episcopal ceremony
and your stone-carved moustache.
Take care of all our dreams;
control the obscurity
of our slumbering prowess
with your relentless heart
and the great ruff of your tail.

*—translated from the Spanish*
*by Alastair Reid*

# CAT ON THE MAT

*J.R.R. Tolkien (1892–1973)*

The fat cat on the mat
        may seem to dream
of nice mice that suffice
        for him, or cream;
but he is free, maybe,
        walks in thought
unbowed, proud, where loud
        roared and fought
his kin, lean and slim,
        or deep in den
in the East feasted on beasts
        and tender men.

The giant lion with iron
        claw in paw,
and huge ruthless tooth
        in gory jaw;
the pard dark-starred
        fleet upon feet,
that oft soft from aloft
        leaps on his meet
where words loom in gloom—
        far now they be
        fierce and free
        and tamed is he;
but fat cat on the mat
kept as pet
he does not forget.

# THE CAT OF CATS

*William Brighty Rands (1823–82)*

I am the cat of cats. I am
    The everlasting cat!
Cunning, and old, and sleek as jam.
    The everlasting cat!

# A MEMORY

*Heinrich Heine (1797–1856)*

It's either the Prize or a terminal worry:
O Wilhelm Wisetzlei, you left in a hurry.
But the cat, the cat is in clover.

The board proved rotten on which you stood
And they fished you out of the water dead.
But the cat, the cat is in clover.

We followed your body, exquisite child;
They buried you in a flowering field.
But the cat, the cat is in clover.

You escaped early, you have been wise
In getting well ere you caught the disease.
But the cat, the cat is in clover.

Year after year, how often have I
Called you to mind with sadness and envy!
But the cat, the cat is in clover!

*—translated from the German
by Francis Golffing*

# THE TOMCAT

*Don Marquis (1878–1937)*

At midnight in the alley
A Tomcat comes to wail,
And he chants the hate of a million years
As he swings his snakey tail.

Malevolent, bony, brindled,
Tiger and devil and bard,
His eyes are coals from the middle of Hell
And his heart is black and hard.

He twists and crouches and capers
And bares his sharp curved claws,
And he sings to the stars of the jungle nights,
Ere cities were, or laws.

Beast from a world primeval,
He and his leaping clan,
When the blotched red moon leers over the roofs,
Give voice to their scorn of man.

He will lie on a rug tomorrow
And lick his silky fur,
And veil the brute in his yellow eyes
And play he's tame, and purr.

But at midnight in the alley
He will crouch again and wail,
And beat the time for his demon's song
with the swing of his demon's tail.

# F R O M  MATTHIAS

*Matthew Arnold (1822–88)*

Rover, with the good brown head,
Great Atossa, they are dead;
Dead, and neither prose nor rhyme
Tells the praises of their prime.
Thou didst know them old and grey,
Know them in their sad decay.
Thou hast seen Atossa sage
Sit for hours beside thy cage;
Thou wouldst chirp, thou foolish bird,
Flutter, chirp—she never stirr'd!
What were now these toys to her?
Down she sank amid her fur;
Eyed thee with a soul resign'd—
And thou deemedst cats were kind!
—Cruel, but composed and bland,
Dumb, inscrutable and grand,
So Tiberius might have sat
Had Tiberius been a cat.

# F R O M  THE DEATH OF A CAT

*Louis MacNeice (1907–63)*

For he was our puck, our miniature lar, he fluttered
Our dovecot of visiting cards, he flicked them askew.
The joker among them who made a full house. As you said,
He was a fine cat. Though how strange to have, as you said later,
Such a personal sense of loss. And looking aside
You said, but unconvincingly: What does it matter?

. . .

    To begin with he was a beautiful object:
Bluecrisp fur with a white collar,
Paws of white velvet, springs of steel,
A Pharaoh's profile, a Krishna's grace,
Tail like a questionmark at a masthead
And eyes dug out of a mine, not the dark
Clouded tarns of a dog's, but cat's eyes—
Light in a rock crystal, light distilled
Before his time and ours, before cats were tame.

    To continue, he was alive and young,
A dancer, incurably male, a clown,
With his gags, his mudras, his entrechats,
His triple bends and his double takes,
Firm as a Rameses in African wonderstone,
Fluid as Krishna chasing the milkmaids,
Who hid under carpets and nibbled at olives,
Attacker of ankles, nonesuch of nonsense,
Indolent, impudent, cat catalytic.

To continue further: if not a person
More than a cipher, if not affectionate
More than indifferent, if not volitive
More than automaton, if not self-conscious
More than mere conscious, if not useful
More than a parasite, if allegorical
More than heraldic, if man-conditioned
More than a gadget, if perhaps a symbol
More than a symbol, if somewhat a proxy
More than a stand-in—was what he was!
A self-contained life, was what he must be
And is not now: more than an object.

And is not now. Spreadeagled on coverlets—
Those are the coverlets, bouncing on chairbacks—
These are the chairs, pirouetting and sidestepping,
Feinting and jabbing, breaking a picture frame—
Here is the picture, tartar and sybarite,
One minute quicksilver, next minute butterballs,
Precise as a fencer, lax as an odalisque,
And in his eyes the light from the mines
One minute flickering, steady the next,
Lulled to a glow or blown to a blaze,
But always the light that was locked in the stone
Before his time and ours; at best semi-precious
All stones of that kind yet, if not precious,
Are more than stones, beautiful objects
But more than objects. While there is light in them.

# THE KING OF CATS
# SENDS A POSTCARD TO HIS WIFE

*Nancy Willard (1936–  )*


Keep your whiskers crisp and clean.
Do not let the mice grow lean.
Do not let yourself grow fat
like a common kitchen cat.

Have you set the kittens free?
Do they sometimes ask for me?
Is our catnip growing tall?
Did you patch the garden wall?

Clouds are gentle walls that hide
gardens on the other side.
Tell the tabby cats I take
all my meals with William Blake,

lunch at noon and tea at four,
served in splendor on the shore
at the tinkling of a bell.
Tell them I am sleeping well.

Tell them I have come so far,
brought by Blake's celestial car,
buffeted by wind and rain,
I may not get home again.

Take this message to my friends.
Say the King of Catnip sends
to the cat who winds his clocks
a thousand sunsets in a box,

to the cat who brings the ice
the shadows of a dozen mice
(serve them with assorted dips
and eat them like potato chips),

and to the cat who guards his door
a net for catching stars, and more
(if with patience he abide):
catnip from the other side.

# THE EPITAPH OF FELIS

*John Jortin (1698–1770)*

*The Epitaph of Felis*
Who departed this life in the year 1757, at the age of 14 years,
11 months and 4 days.

I most gentle of cats through long-drawn sickness aweary,
    Bidding a last farewell, turn to the waters below.
Quietly smiling to me says Queen Proserpina, "Welcome!
    Thine are the groves of the blest: thine the Elysian suns."
If I deserve so well, O merciful Queen of the Silent,
    Let me come back one night, homeward returning again,
Crossing the threshold again in the ear of the master to murmur,
    "Even when over the Styx, Felis is faithful to thee."

*—translated from the Latin*
*by Samuel Courtauld*

# A CAT

*Edward Thomas (1878–1917)*

She had a name among the children;
But no one loved though someone owned
Her, locked her out of doors at bedtime
And had her kittens duly drowned.

In Spring, nevertheless, this cat
Ate blackbirds, thrushes, nightingales,
And birds of bright voice and plume and flight,
As well as scraps from neighbours' pails.

I loathed and hated her for this;
One speckle on a thrush's breast
Was worth a million such; and yet
She lived long, till God gave her rest.

# ON A CAT, AGEING

*Sir Alexander Gray (1882–1968)*

He blinks upon the hearth-rug,
And yawns in deep content,
Accepting all the comforts
That Providence has sent.

Louder he purrs, and louder,
In one glad hymn of praise
For all the night's adventures,
For quiet restful days.

Life will go on forever,
With all that cat can wish,
Warmth and the glad procession
of fish and milk and fish.

Only—the thought disturbs him—
He's noticed once or twice,
The times are somehow breeding
A nimbler race of mice.

# FROST EYEBROWS

*after Wang T'ung-kuei (seventeenth century)*

Frost Eyebrows was the favorite cat
Of the Chia-ching Emperor of the Ming;
Her coat was pale blue,
But her eyebrows were as white as jade.
And truly Frost Eyebrows
Was herself a skilled courtier.
Where the Emperor wished to go, she led;
Whom the Emperor wished to see, she approached.
Her beauty was unsurpassed;
She seemed deep and wise,
Majestic as the dragons
On His Majesty's embroidered robes.
Frost Eyebrows slept every night on the Emperor's bed,
And when once she did not awaken,
The Emperor made her a tomb on Longevity Mountain,
And set up a stone:
Here Lies a Veritable Dragon.

—F.B.

# TO WINKY

*Amy Lowell (1874–1925)*

Cat, Cat,
What are you?
Son, through a thousand generations, of the black leopards
Padding among the sprigs of young bamboo:
Descendant of many removals from the white panthers
Who crouch by night under the loquat-trees?
You crouch under the orange begonias,
And your eyes are green
With the violence of murder,
Or half-closed and stealthy
Like your sheathed claws.
Slowly, slowly,
You rise and stretch
In a glossiness of beautiful curves,
Of muscles fluctuating under black, glazed hair.

Cat,
You are a strange creature.
You sit on your haunches
And yawn
But when you leap
I can almost hear the whine
of a released string,
And I look to see its flaccid shaking
In the place whence you sprang.

You carry your tail as a banner,
Slowly it passes my chair,
But when I look for you, you are on the table
Moving easily among the most delicate porcelains.
Your food is a matter of importance
And you are insistent on having
Your wants attended to,
And yet you will eat a bird and its feathers
Apparently without injury.

In the night, I hear you crying,
But if I try to find you
There are only the shadows of rhododendron leaves
Brushing the ground.
When you come in out of the rain,
All wet and with your tail full of burrs,
You fawn on me in coils and subtleties;
But once you are dry
You leave me with a gesture of inconceivable impudence,
Conveyed by the vanishing quirk of your tail
As you slide through the open door.

You walk as a king scorning his subjects;
You flirt with me as a concubine in robes of silk.
Cat,
I am afraid of your poisonous beauty,
I have seen you torturing a mouse.
Yet when you lie purring in my lap
I forget everything but how soft you are,
And it is only when I feel your claws open upon my hand
That I remember—
Remember a puma lying out on a branch above my head
Years ago.

Shall I choke you, Cat,
Or kiss you?
Really I do not know.

# NATIVITÉ

*André Spire (1868–1966)*


*Knowest thou the time when the wild goats of rock bring forth? Or canst thou mark*
*when the hinds calve? They bring forth their young and they are delivered of their sorrows.*
*—Job*

The cat lies on her back,
Tender eyed, open mouthed,
Pale curved tongue rose-tipped . . .

The cat gasps in the night . . .
A star in the midst of branches
Gleams cold, like the rings
Of a glow-worm moving through leaves.

Now tiny heads and paws swarm
On the cat's belly softly warm.

No wind. A leaf falls.

*—translated from the French*
*by Stanley Burnshaw*

# MILK FOR THE CAT

*Harold Monro (1879–1932)*

When the tea is brought at five o'clock,
And all the neat curtains are drawn with care,
The little black cat with bright green eyes
Is suddenly purring there.

At first she pretends, having nothing to do,
She has come in merely to blink by the grate,
But, though tea may be late and the milk may be sour,
She is never late.

And presently her agate eyes
Take a soft large milky haze,
And her independent casual glance
Becomes a stiff hard gaze.

Then she stamps her claws or lifts her ears
Or twists her tail and begins to stir,
Till suddenly all her lithe body becomes
One breathing trembling purr.

The children eat and wriggle and laugh;
The two old ladies stroke their silk:
But the cat is grown small and thin with desire,
Transformed to a creeping lust for milk.

The white saucer like some full moon descends
At last from the clouds of the table above;
She sighs and dreams and thrills and glows,
Transfigured with love.

She nestles over the shining rim,
Buries her chin in the creamy sea;
Her tail hangs loose; each drowsy paw
Is doubled under each bending knee.

A long dim ecstasy holds her life;
Her world is an infinite shapeless white,
Till her tongue has curled the last holy drop,
Then she sinks back into the night.

Draws and dips her body to heap
Her sleepy nerves in the great arm-chair,
Lies defeated and buried deep
Three or four hours unconscious there.

# MICE BEFORE MILK

from "The Manciple's Tale"

*Geoffrey Chaucer (1343–1400)*


Lat take a cat and fostre hym wel with milk
And tendre flessch and make his couche of silk,
And lat hym seen a mouse go by the wal,
Anon he weyvith milk and flessch and al,
And every deyntee that is in that hous,
Suich appetit he hath to ete a mous.

# MOON

*William Jay Smith (1918– )*

I have a white cat whose name is Moon;
He eats catfish from a wooden spoon,
And sleeps till five each afternoon.

Moon goes out when the moon is bright
And sycamore trees are spotted white
To sit and stare in the dead of night.

Beyond still water cries a loon,
Through mulberry leaves peers a wild baboon
And in Moon's eyes I see the moon.

# MOTHER CAT

*John Montague (1929–   )*

The mother cat
opens her claws
like petals

bends her spine
to expose her
battery of tits

where her young
toothless snouts
screwed eyes

on which light
cuffs mild
paternal blows

jostle & cry
for position
except one

so boneless
and frail it
pulls down

air, not milk.
Wan little scut
you are already

set for death
never getting
a say against

the warm circle
of your mother's
breast, as she

arches voluptuously
in the pleasure
of giving life

to those who
claim it, bit-
ten navel cords

barely dry,
already fierce
at the trough.

# CAT~GODDESSES

*Robert Graves (1895–1985)*


A perverse habit of cat-goddesses—
Even the blackest of them, black as coals
Save for a new moon blazing on each breast,
With coral tongues and beryl eyes like lamps,
Long-legged, pacing three by three in nines—
This obstinate habit is to yield themselves,
In verisimilar love-ecstasies,
To tatter-eared and slinking alley-toms
No less below the common run of cats
Than they above it; which they do for spite,
To provoke jealousy—not the least abashed
By such gross-headed, rabbit-coloured litters
As soon they shall be happy to desert.

# THE EMPRESS'S CAT

*after Chang Tsu (660–741)*

Long ago, the Empress Wu Tse-t'ien,
Seeking to show that where Buddha's law prevails
All violence and strife must cease,
Ordered that a kitten and a bird
Be trained to eat from the same dish.
The bird, a parrot, was clever and playful;
The cat, in turn, was placid and mild.
And indeed they did take their food together.
Yet when Censor P'eng exhibited them
To the officials at court
To manifest the transforming benevolence
Of Her Majesty's rule,
The cat became nervous, and bit
Her erstwhile comrade to death:
Thus in view of all could be concealed
Neither the violence of the cat
Nor the ambition of the ruler.

—*F.B.*

# FEMME ET CHATTE

*Paul Verlaine (1844–96)*

They were just playing, lady and cat,
Their sport was a marvelous sight:
White hand, white paw, tit-for-tat,
In the shadow of gathering night.

She tried to conceal (to little avail)
Beneath gloves of the finest black net
A set of deadly agate-hard nails
Honed sharper than razors can whet.

And sweet as sugar, or so it seemed,
The other tucked claws away too;
But let's give the devil, as ever, his due . . .

And suddenly in the boudoir, where
A froth of laughter had filled the air,
Four dazzling points of phosphor gleamed.

> —*translated from the French*
> *by F.B.*

# TO A PERSIAN CAT

*F.C.W. Hiley (nineteenth century)*

So dear, so dainty, so demure,
So charming in whate'er position;
By race the purest of the pure,
A little cat of high condition:
Her coat lies not in trim-kept rows
Of carpet-like and vulgar sleekness:
But like a ruffled sea it grows
Of wavy grey (my special weakness):
She vexes not the night with squalls
That make one seize a boot and throw it:
She joins in no unseemly brawls
(At least she never lets me know it!);
She never bursts in at the door
In manner boisterous and loud:
But silently along the floor
She passes, like a little cloud.
Then, opening wide her amber eyes,
Puts an inquiring nose up—
Sudden upon my knee she flies,
Then purrs and tucks her little toes up.

# THE SPRING IS A CAT

*Jang-hi Lee (1902–28)*


On a cat's fur soft as pollen,
The mild Spring's fragrance lingers.

In a cat's eyes round as golden bells,
The mad Spring's flame glows.

On a cat's gently closed lips,
The soft Spring's drowsiness lies.

On a cat's sharp whiskers,
The green Spring's life dances.

*—translated from the Korean*
*by Chang-soo Koh*

# BLACK CAT

*Rainer Maria Rilke (1875–1926)*

A ghost, though invisible, still is like a place
your sight can knock on, echoing; but here
within this thick black pelt, your strongest gaze
will be absorbed and utterly disappear:

just as a raving madman, when nothing else
can ease him, charges into his dark night
howling, pounds on the padded wall, and feels
the rage being taken in and pacified.

She seems to hide all looks that have ever fallen
into her, so that, like an audience,
she can look them over, menacing and sullen,
and curl to sleep with them.   But all at once

as if awakened, she turns her face to yours;
and with a shock, you see yourself, tiny,
inside the golden amber of her eyeballs
suspended, like a prehistoric fly.

*—translated from the German*
*by Stephen Mitchell*

# ODE

ON THE DEATH OF A FAVORITE CAT,
DROWNED IN A TUB OF GOLDFISHES

*Thomas Gray (1716–71)*

'Twas on a lofty vase's side,
Where China's gayest art had dyed
   The azure flowers that blow;
Demurest of the tabby kind,
The pensive Selima, reclined,
   Gazed on the lake below.

Her conscious tail her joy declared;
The fair round face, the snowy beard,
   The velvet of her paws,
Her coat, that with the tortoise vies,
Her ears of jet, and emerald eyes.
   She saw, and purred applause.

Still had she gazed; but 'midst the tide
Two angel forms were seen to glide,
   The genii of the stream:
Their scaly armor's Tyrian hue
Through richest purple to the view
   Betrayed a golden gleam.

The hapless nymph with wonder saw:
A whisker first and then a claw,
    With many an ardent wish,
She stretched in vain to reach the prize.
What female heart can gold despise?
    What cat's averse to fish?

Presumptuous maid! with looks intent
Again she stretched, again she bent.
    Nor knew the gulf between.
(Malignant Fate sat by and smiled)
The slippery verge her feet beguiled,
    She tumbled headlong in.

Eight times emerging from the flood
She mewed to every watery god,
    Some speedy aid to send.
No dolphin came, no Nereid stirred;
Nor cruel Tom, nor Susan heard;
    A favorite has no friend!

From hence, ye beauties, undeceived,
Know, one false step is ne'er retrieved,
    And be with caution bold.
Not all that tempts your wandering eyes
And heedless hearts, is lawful prize;
    Nor all that glisters, gold.

# NATURAL SELECTION

*Jess Williamson (1942–   )*


Chickadees should never
enter buildings.
Impelled perhaps by an errant
gene for boldness
one did, and came
to an evolutionary
dead end
in my woodshed.
A grey blur,
pitiless claws:
my cat was on it
in no time.
Afterwards only
a scatter of feathers
marked the spot.

# THE CATS OF ST. NICHOLAS

*George Seferis (1900–71)*

"That's the Cape of Cats ahead," the captain said to me,
pointing through the mist to a low stretch of shore,
the beach deserted; it was Christmas Day—
". . . and there, in the distance to the west, is where Aphrodite rose
        out of the waves;
they call the place 'Greek's Rock.'
Left ten degrees rudder!"
She had Salome's eyes, the cat I lost a year ago;
and old Ramazan, how he would look death square in the eyes,
whole days long in the snow of the East,
under the frozen sun,
days long square in the eyes: the young hearth god.
Don't stop, traveler.
"Left ten degrees rudder," muttered the helmsman.

. . . my friend, though, might well have stopped short,
now between ships,
shut up in a small house with pictures,
searching for windows behind the frames.
The ship's bell struck
like a coin from some vanished city
that brings to mind, as it falls,
alms from another time.
"It's strange," the captain said.
"That bell—given what day it is—
reminded me of another one, the monastery bell.
A monk told me the story,
a half-mad monk, a kind of dreamer.

"It was during the great drought,
forty years without rain,
the whole island devastated,
people dying and snakes giving birth.
This cape had millions of snakes
fat as a man's leg
and full of poison.
In those days the monastery of St. Nicholas
was held by the monks of St. Basil,
and they couldn't go out to work their fields,
couldn't put their flocks to pasture.
In the end they were saved by the cats they raised.
Every day at dawn a bell would strike
and an army of cats would move into battle.
They'd fight the day long,
until the bell sounded for the evening feed.
Supper done, the bell would sound again
and they'd go to battle through the night.
They say it was a marvellous sight to see them,
some lame, some blind, others missing
a nose, an ear, their hides in shreds.
So to the sound of four bells a day
months went by, years, season after season.
Wildly obstinate, always wounded,
they annihilated the snakes; but in the end they disappeared;
they just couldn't take in that much poison.

Like a sunken ship
they left no trace on the surface:
not a meow, not even a bell.
Steady as you go!
Poor devils, what could they do,
fighting like that day and night, drinking
the poisonous blood of those snakes?
Generations of poison, centuries of poison."
"Steady as you go," indifferently echoed the helmsman.

—*translated from the Greek*
*by Edmund Keeley and Philip Sherrard*

# THE CATS OF KILKENNY

*Anonymous*

There once were two cats of Kilkenny,
Each thought there was one cat too many.
So they fought and they fit,
And they scratched and they bit,
Till, excepting their nails
And the tips of their tails,
Instead of two cats, there weren't any.

# CURIOSITY

may have killed the cat; more likely
the cat was just unlucky, or else curious
to see what death was like, having no cause
to go on licking paws, or fathering
litter on litter of kittens, predictably.

Nevertheless, to be curious
is dangerous enough.   To distrust
what is always said, what seems,
to ask odd questions, interfere in dreams,
leave home, smell rats, have hunches
do not endear cats to those doggy circles
where well-smelt baskets, suitable wives, good lunches
are the order of things, and where prevails
much wagging of incurious heads and tails.

Face it.   Curiosity
will not cause us to die—
only lack of it will.
Never to want to see
the other side of the hill
or that improbable country
where living is an idyll
(although a probable hell)
would kill us all.
Only the curious
have, if they live, a tale
worth telling at all.

Dogs say cats love too much, are irresponsible,
are changeable, marry too many wives,
desert their children, chill all dinner tables
with tales of their nine lives.
Well, they are lucky.   Let them be
nine-lived and contradictory,
curious enough to change, prepared to pay
the cat price, which is to die
and die again and again,
each time with no less pain.
A cat minority of one
is all that can be counted on
to tell the truth.   And what cats have to tell
on each return from hell
is this:   that dying is what the living do,
that dying is what the loving do,
and that dead dogs are those who do not know
that dying is what, to live, each has to do.

*Alastair Reid (1926–    )*

# THE SINGLE CREATURE

*W. H. Auden (1907–73)*

DOG    The single creature leads a partial life,
            Man by his mind, and by his nose the hound;
            He needs the deep emotions I can give,
            I scent in him a vaster hunting ground.

CATS    Like calls to like, to share is to relieve,
            And sympathy the root bears love the flower;
            He feels in us, and we in him perceive
            A common passion for the lonely hour.

CATS    We move in our apartness and our pride,
            About the decent dwellings he has made:
DOG    In all his walks I follow at his side,
            His faithful servant and his loving shade.

# POEM

*William Carlos Williams (1883–1963)*

As the cat
climbed over
the top of

the jamcloset
first the right
forefoot

carefully
then the hind
stepped down

into the pit of
the empty
flower pot

# LAST WORDS TO A DUMB FRIEND

*Thomas Hardy (1840–1928)*

Pet was never mourned as you,
Purrer of the spotless hue,
Plumy tail, and wistful gaze,
While you humoured our queer ways,
Or outshrilled your morning call
Up the stairs and through the hall—
Foot suspended in its fall—
While, expectant, you would stand
Arched, to meet the stroking hand;
Till your way you chose to wend
Yonder, to your tragic end.

Never another pet for me!
Let your place all vacant be;
Better blankness day by day
Than companion torn away.
Better bid his memory fade,
Better blot each mark he made,
Selfishly escape distress
By contrived forgetfulness,
Than preserve his prints to make
Every morn and eve an ache.

From the chair whereon he sat
Sweep his fur, nor wince thereat;
Rake his little pathways out
Mid the bushes roundabout;
Smooth away his talons' mark
From the claw-worn pine-tree bark,
Where he climbed as dusk embrowned
Waiting us who loitered round.

Strange it is this speechless thing,
Subject to our mastering,
Subject for his life and food
To our gift, and time, and mood;
Timid pensioner of us Powers,
His existence ruled by ours,
Should—by crossing at a breath
Into safe and shielded death,
By the merely taking hence
Of his insignificance—
Loom as largened to the sense,
Shape as part, above man's will,
Of the Imperturbable.

As a prisoner, flight debarred,
Exercising in a yard,
Still retain I, troubled, shaken,
Mean estate, by him forsaken;
And this home, which scarcely took
Impress from his little look,
By his faring to the Dim,
Grows all eloquent of him.

Housemate, I can think you still
Bounding to the window-sill,
Over which I vaguely see
Your small mound beneath the tree,
Showing in the autumn shade
That you moulder where you played.

# DREAM:

*Raphael Rudnik (1938–   )*

A cat on gold-glowing black coals,
Like an enormous untouched bud
In the wincing glare,—must breathe air like hot towels.
Every hair of the black and white coat
Turns to gold, but does not burn. Eye a seeing leaf,
Sees me, blinks—as if I were beyond belief.
Then shooting claws of fire shine it red.
The cat sits afloat there, safe and alone. And wills
Me to understand it catches, kills
Something weak like the fear-ball in my throat.

I saw it as a true, imperfect picture
Of the blurred nakedness passionate friends can offer.
Growing smaller, and the fire seemed to be far,
Pale and shiny as a scar, insane, particular . . .

# STARS

*Oktay Rifat (1914–    )*


Near the book a notebook
near the notebook a glass
near the glass a child
in the child's hand a cat.
and far away stars stars.

*—translated from the Turkish
by Taner Baybars*

# THE CAT

*Charles Baudelaire (1821–67)*

1

Along the hallways of my thought,
As if at home, there prowls a cat,
A strong, sweet, charming, splendid cat.
He mews: the sound is barely caught,

So soft and diffident its tone.
Cries of contentment or complaint
A throaty resonance contain,
A charm, a secret of their own.

A voice that slakes and saturates
The deepest shaded parts of me
And fills my soul like poetry;
Like magic, it rejuvenates.

It lulls to sleep my cruel malaise,
Contains all ecstasy as well;
There is no need of words to tell
The long complexities of phrase.

No bow could rasp across my heart,
Though perfect instrument it be,
And make it throb more royally,
More resonant in every part,

Than does your voice, mysterious,
Seraphic cat, eccentric cat;
An angel's song is in your throat,
So subtle and harmonious.

2

His fur is dappled brown and blond,
And has such sweet perfume, last night
When I had touched him with one light
Caress, my hand became embalmed.

He is the soul of our abode:
the judge, the king, the inspiration
Of everything in his small nation.
Perhaps a demon, is he God?

When, as by a magnet's spell,
This cherished cat has caught my eyes,
Then, docilely, to analyze
They turn and gaze into my self,

With what astonishment I see
The fire within his living pupils,
Lighted beacons, living opals,
Which contemplate me fixedly!

—*translated from the French*
*by William H. Crosby*

# THE WHITE CAT OF TRENARREN

*A. L. Rowse (1903–    )*
*(For Beryl Cloke)*


He was a mighty hunter in his youth
At Polmear all day on the mound, on the pounce
For anything moving, rabbit or bird or mouse—
   *My cat and I grow old together.*

After a day's hunting he'd come into the house
Delicate ears stuck all with fleas.
At Trenarren I've heard him sigh with pleasure
After a summer's day in the long-grown leas—
   *My cat and I grow old together.*

When I was a child I played all day,
With only a little cat for companion,
At solitary games of my own invention
Under the table or up in the green bay—
   *My cat and I grow old together.*

When I was a boy I wandered the roads
Up to the downs by gaunt Carn Grey,
Wrapt in a dream at end of day,
All round me the moor, below me the bay—
   *My cat and I grow old together.*

Now we are too often apart, yet
Turning out of Central Park into the Plaza,
Or walking Michigan Avenue against the lake-wind,
I see a little white shade in the shrubbery
Of far-off Trenarren, never far from my mind—
   *My cat and I grow old together.*

When I come home from too much travelling,
Cautiously he comes out of his lair to my call,
Receives me at first with a shy reproach
At long absence to him incomprehensible—
*My cat and I grow old together.*

Incapable of much or long resentment,
He scratches at my door to be let out
In early morning in the ash moonlight,
Or red dawn breaking through Mother Bond's spinney—
*My cat and I grow old together.*

No more frisking as of old,
Or chasing his shadow over the lawn,
But a dignified old person, tickling
His nose against twig or flower in the border,
Until evening falls and bed-time's in order,
Unable to keep eyes open any longer
He waits for me to carry him upstairs
To nestle all night snug at foot of bed—
*My cat and I grow old together.*

Careful of his licked and polished appearance,
Ears like shell-whorls pink and transparent,
White plume waving proudly over the paths,
Against a background of sea and blue hydrangeas—
*My cat and I grow old together.*

# CATS

*Fazil Hüsnü Dağlarca (1914–  )*

The widow's
Cat
Feels
Warmer
Than the bride's.

*—translated from the Turkish*
*by Murat Nemet-Nejat*

# DIAMOND CUT DIAMOND

*Ewart Milne (1903–87)*

Two cats
One up a tree
One under the tree
The cat up the tree is he
The cat under the tree is she
The tree is a witch elm, just incidentally.
He takes no notice of she, she takes no notice of he
He stares at the woolly clouds passing, she stares at the tree.
There's been a lot written about cats, by Old Possum, Yeats and
Company
But not Alfred de Musset or Lord Tennyson or Poe or anybody
Wrote about one cat under, and one cat up, a tree.
God knows why this should be left for me
Except I like cats as cats be
Especially one cat up
And one cat under
A witch elm
Tree.

# THE LOST CAT

*E. V. Rieu (1887–1972)*

She took a last and simple meal when there were none to see
        her steal—
    A jug of cream upon the shelf, a fish prepared for
        dinner;
And now she walks a distant street with delicately sandalled
        feet,
    And no one gives her much to eat or weeps to see her
        thinner.

O my beloved come again, come back in joy, come back in pain,
    To end our searching with a mew, or with a purr our
        grieving;
And you shall have for lunch or tea whatever fish swim in the
        sea
    And all the cream that's meant for me—and not a word
        of thieving!

# LULLABY FOR THE CAT

*Elizabeth Bishop (1911–79)*

Minnow, go to sleep and dream
    Close your great big eyes;
Round your bed Events prepare
    The pleasantest surprise.

Darling Minnow, drop that frown,
    Just cooperate,
Not a kitten shall be drowned
    In the Marxist State.

Joy and Love will both be yours,
    Minnow, don't be glum.
Happy days are coming soon—
    Sleep, and let them come.

# APARTMENT CATS

*Thom Gunn (1929–    )*

The Girls wake, stretch, and pad up to the door.
    They rub my leg and purr;
    One sniffs around my shoe,
    Rich with an outside smell,
    The other rolls back on the floor—
White bib exposed, and stomach of soft fur.

Now, more awake, they re-enact Ben Hur
    Along the corridor,
    Wheel, gallop; as they do,
    Their noses twitching still,
    Their eyes get wild, their bodies tense,
Their usual prudence seemingly withdraws.

And then they wrestle: parry, lock of paws,
    Blind hug of close defense,
    Tail-thump, and smothered mew.
    If either, though, feels claws,
    She abruptly rises, knowing well
How to stalk off in wise indifference.

# CHARLEMAGNE

*from* THE GOLDEN GATE

*Vikram Seth (1952–   )*


Why scratch a scratching post when trousers
Present themselves? Why bite a bone?
Why hunt mere mice like lesser mousers
When, having gnawed the telephone
Receiver when you sensed the presage
Of an impending urgent message
From John's curt boss, who can't afford
To waste time, you can short the cord?
Why vex yourself with paltry matters
When a report named *Bipartite
Para-Models of Missile Flight*
Can casually be torn to tatters?
And why, in short, crave vapid food
When you can drink your foe's heart's blood?

Blood! This is no farfetched analogy.
In this connection it's germane
To note his psychic genealogy:
The warrior blood of Charlemagne
Brims with—a bonus for a rhymer—
The hunting spirit of Selima,
The wits of Fritz, the fierce élan
Of the exultant Pangur Bán.
The grand Tiberian Atossa
And the electric Cat Jeoffry
Are honored in a pedigree
Long as your arm and high as Ossa.
I list these but to illustrate
The hybrid vigor of the great.

# CAT AT NIGHT

*Adrien Stoutenburg (1916–93)*

The cat in moonlight
takes his shadow with him
over the fence
and loses it under the cottonwoods.

# FIVE EYES

*Walter de la Mare (1873–1956)*

In Hans' old mill his three black cats
Watch his bins for thieving rats.
Whisker and claw, they crouch in the night,
Their five eyes smouldering green and bright:
Squeaks from the flour sacks, squeaks from where
The cold wind stirs on the empty stair,
Squeaking and scampering, everywhere.
Then down they pounce, now in, now out,
At whisking tail, and sniffing snout;
While lean old Hans he snores away
Till peep of light at break of day;
Then up he climbs to his creaking mill,
Out come his cats all grey with meal—Jekkel, and Jessup, and one-eyed Jill.

# GORBY AND THE RATS

*Obeyd-i-Zàkànì (c. 1330–71)*

Long long ago
when God was, for without Him nothing was,
and Time had just begun
Heaven decreed a cat should dwell
in a city called Kirmàn.

The cat was Gorby
and his reputation caused great alarm
throughout the land of Persia.
His tail was borrowed from a lion
his paws were golden eagles' claws
his chest a silver shield
and every whisker was a sword.

Once, it is said, four lions
dining on honest prey
hearing this dragon-cat roar seven miles away
left their feast unfinished
and with prudence and in peace
slunk
     silently
          away.

In fact
he was no purring pusillanimous puss.
HE was a CAT, whose paws were the law
and THAT was THAT.

When Gorby was hungry he used to hide
in a cellar the rats monopolised,
and like a robber in a park
he'd crouch behind full jars of wine
and inside vats
waiting to pounce on well-wined rats.

One day
a noisy rat jumped from the cellar wall
dipped his nose and drank,
and drank
and drank his fill
until he thought his squeak a lion's roar.
"Where's that cataleptic kit,
that feline fraud," he growled,
"I'll knot his whiskers, nip his neck
and stuff his hide with straw,
or is pretty little fluffkin scaredy-cat
afraid to meet on the open battle-floor?"

Gorby, still silent, yawned and filed his claws.

Suddenly he pounced, like a tiger on a mountain-goat.
"You're doomed," he miaowed, and grabbed the drunkard's throat.

The rat, his larynx almost severed, whispered, "Gorby dear
your eyes are lanterns leading us to Paradise. Your fur . . .
Forgive me, I have dined too well for humble folk.
Sweet wine has soured my words and fouled my soul
but I am innocent. It was the wine that spoke."

"Rats," said Gorby, "your tongue has never tasted truth,
and I am deaf to lies.
I heard you call me 'Ali-cat,' and worse,
you paper-rat, all filth and fleas,
muscle-man indeed! I'll Musselman you!
I'll weary your wife with waiting.
She'll need another mate now."

In short, cat ate rat, then,
conforming to the ritual laws
washed his whiskers, face, and claws,
and with all humility
went to the mosque and prayed:

*Creator of the Universe,*
*this cat repents with contrite heart*
*the Muslim blood he used to shed*
*in rats he tore apart.*
*Be Clement, be Merciful,*
*I'll wrong them no more*
*and here renounce all ratting*
*and promise alms to the poor.*

By Heaven's whim
a hidden mosque-rat overheard
puss's promised virtue to his Lord
and before the cat could change his mind
the rat had hustled off to spread the news
to all ratkind.

"Gorby has repented. Gorby has repented.
I saw him in the mosque today
like a pious mullah, beads in paw,
wailing and praying
eyes cast down towards the floor.
O Allah is Compassionate and Merciful is His Name,
dear puss is one of us again."

They pranced and danced and sang,
"Dear puss is one of us again,"
and drank and drank,
". . . is pussulman again."

Then up stepped The Seven
the noblest of them all, and said,
"Our love for puss is such
we nominate each other
to carry a feast to his celestial hall."

One brought wine,
the next, a whole roast lamb,
another, sweet raisins from his estate,
the fourth, seven dates as big as mice,
the fifth, a bag of fragrant cheese
which was to have been his New Year's feast.
Another thought yoghurt would bring peace
to his digestion,
and the seventh, proudest of them all,
carried above his turbaned brow
a bowl of great price, heaped with pilàw
nightingales' wings
almonds and rice
decked with sweet lemon rind and spice;
and murmuring salaams in puss's praise
they marched to the palace
for audience with the cat.

There they were hastily ushered in.
They bowed, fell reverently upon their paws
and squeaked:
"Our heads are gravel beneath your silken paws
our souls but footstools at your feet—
taste these slight refreshments, accept our humble pie,
so we may praise your goodness
and serve you till we die."

"'Tis true," the cat replied, "our Holy Book doth say,
'Heaven rewards the pious and the faithful,' and I,
as only Allah knows, have fasted long enough to please Him,
for Behold!—my Reward!
Here you are—a portion
of the Bounty I am worthy of . . .
but pardon me,
wondering how to serve you best
I quite forgot myself.
Your presence is my soul's true nourishment.
Come near my dears and sit by me.
*O Allah! What fools these morsels be!*
Come closer, beside me, on this sofa.
*Near's too far—I wish you were all inside me.*"

The rats advanced, each a quivering willow-branch.
"Now," said Gorby, "let us prey,"
and springing like a lion, grabbed the nearest five
two per paw, while one
hung loosely from his jaw—alive.

Tailless but with a tale to tell
the two survivors fled.
"That cat," they said, "has slain
five princes of our realm
and all you do is murmur:
'Peace be upon you, peace';
FIVE, belovèd of our clan
torn apart while still alive.
May death be their release
and SHAME, everlasting shame—YOUR only glory."

And dusting themselves with sands of woe
they blacked their brows
dipped their tails in sorrow's mead, and howled,
"To the Capitol, and there we'll tell our King."

King Rat, aloof upon his throne
saw them coming from afar
and wondering what they wanted
ordered the palace gates slightly ajar.

The rats came in, bowed in unison and sang:

*O Royal Rodent, King of Kings*
*for whom all rodents pray*
*five princeling rats, five rodent lives*
*were swallowed up today.*


Rex rattus! Rex rattus!
Our humble hearts are sad.
O Monarch of all ages
that feline has gone mad.
He used to snatch but one a year
and now he swallows five
yet still proclaims his piety
to those he's left alive.


The Royal Anger rose
and clothed its words in pride.
(Here's vengeance for your story-books.)
"THAT CAT MUST DIE!
or thirty thousand Mussulmen
shall know the reason why."

Within a week the Palace Guard
armed with lances, arrows, slings, and swords
were joined by loyal peasant hordes
from Khurasàn and Resht:
packrats with catgut for catapults and kitbags for cats
rattletrap and samovars, and poisoned snacks.

The army ready, "Wisdom of the Ages,"
an elder in the Royal Ratinue
squeaked sagely,
"We must despatch a diplomat
with a knack for rhatoric to tell that cat
IT'S WAR OR SUBMISSION,"
and soon
an envoy had scurried to Gorby Hall
to gently breathe his mission.

"His Majesty orders his humble envoy, me,
to beg your presence at his court, professing loyalty,
and bids me to inform you
his army numbers thousands, whose loyalty is sure;
Alas! O lustrous furry one,
IT'S FEALTY or WAR."

"Cat-fodder," snarled Gorby, "go away.
I am in command here, and in Kirmàn I stay,"
and secretly mustered an army of cats,
regiments from Isfahan and Princes from Yazd.

By the great salt desert marched the rats
across mountain passes rode the cats
to the open Plains of Fàrs,
and there both armies met and fought
paw to paw in battle, like heroes from the past.

In every corner of the field unnumbered lie the dead,
as vanguards fall, reserves stand still—
no space for lances, horse or shield,
and nowhere else to tread.

Then right to the center the Feline Guard attacks
as a regiment of rodents turns tail in its tracks.
Confusion and chaos    havoc and doubt
as cat after cat wins every bout
and many a rat is routed.

Then suddenly arose          a cry of valor
    "The cat is down!"    All Praise to Allah.
            "Rally, rats! Rally!"


There lay Gorby groaning on the ground
        his stallion's heel nipped by a rat
    who swore to bring him down.
            Puss to dust. Alas!
            There Gorby lay
        groaning several lives away
            on the Plain of Fàrs.


    "Catch him! Bind him! Truss him up!"
        squeaked seven rat-lion-cubs.
        "Tie his paws with string,
    tie 'em tight and mind his claws,
            then WE
        will take him to our King."
            (Loud applause.)

They danced and pranced and beat the drum of joy
until they reached the court.

And there, King Rat, seeing the cat was safely tied
scowled and shouted:
"Foul inhuman beast! You lied!
You ate my army, you greedy thing,
and worse—without the Royal Permission."

"Alas," sighed Gorby,
"my face is black with shame and sin,
my soulless soul now pleads and craves
your Royal Renown for Clemency
to save my worthless skin.
Hear my purr for pardon, Lord.
Hear my purrrrrrrrr."
His words were wet with weeping.

"To the gibbet with that dog of a cat,"
the King shouted.
"In recompense for all the noble necks he broke
I myself will ride the Royal Elephant
to watch him swing
and die."

And surrounded by his army
fore and aft
he rode in triumph through the town
to hear the music of his citizens
who cheered and laughed.

And there in the market-place tied to the gallows
stood Gorby, miaowing and caterwauling sorrows.

"What! Do I hear a miaow from that black Kirmàni cow?
Is he still alive, when I decreed THAT CAT MUST DIE,
AND NOW?"

Some edged back by nudging others on.
Their chatter soon became a murmur,
till all had swallowed silence and were dumb.
Not a rat stirred.
Not a rat in all the rout
dared step up and hang the cat,
not to win all Persia.

The King, sorrowed by their shame
and furious at their fear
quivered angrily,
"What! Are we starved of heroes here?
You rattle-tattle rodent bipeds,
you slinking sewer rats.
May every feline in Kirmàn
feast off you tonight."
And stepping forward, single-pawed
he raised his sword
to cut the cat in two.

When Gorby saw the King of Rats
he suddenly became a dragoned-lion again:
his courage boiled, the cauldron of his fury spilled,
he tore his cords asunder,
spread his golden eagles' claws
unsheathed each whiskered quill and sword
and levelled every rat
so none would rise again—
except as dust.

Which ends my tale. The army fled.
King Rat deserted.
Howdah and kingdom tumbled down,
while I,
steeped in the wine of wonder
asked the meaning of this yarn.
"The meaning's clear," the poet said,
"if you are wise enough to see it.
It is . . ." But then, alas,
came the allotted span.
Allah called,


our poet heard his name:


𝕺 𝕭 𝕮 𝖄 𝕯


and passed away.


. . . and as in every chestnut lies
Truth's Kernel—so in every tale.


—*translated from the Persian
by Omar Pound*

# THE DESIRE TO BE IN TWO PLACES AT ONCE

*Charles Henri Ford (1913–   )*


Stones watch the sea like cats:    the stone of sleep
pulls me away from the dream that creeps
like the cat to the shore:    there hops the fish,
I; stone and cat:    both mine to wonder at.

# THE HAPPY CAT

*Randall Jarrell (1914–65)*

The cat's asleep; I whisper *kitten*
Till he stirs a little and begins to purr—
He doesn't wake. Today out on the limb
(The limb he thinks he can't climb down from)
He mewed until I heard him in the house.
I climbed up to get him down: he mewed.
What he says and what he sees are limited.
My own response is even more constricted.
I think, "It's lucky; what you have is too."
What do you have except—well, me?
I joke about it but it's not a joke:
The house and I are all he remembers.
Next month how will he guess that it is winter
And not just entropy, the universe
Plunging at last into its cold decline?
I cannot think of him without a pang.
Poor rumpled thing, why don't you see
That you have no more, really, than a man?
Men aren't happy: why are you?

# CAT

*William Jay Smith (1918–    )*


Cats are not at all like people,
>Cats are Cats.

People wear stockings and sweaters,
Overcoats, mufflers, and hats.
Cats wear nothing: they lie by the fire
For twenty-four hours if they desire.
They do NOT rush out of the office,
They do NOT have interminable chats,
They do NOT play Old Maid and Checkers,
They do NOT wear bright yellow spats.

People, of course, will always be people,
>But Cats are Cats.